The Sea
for Eugenia Lynch

The story of Norfolk's unknown
Victorian photographers

Janis Austin, writer, researcher and photographic historian

Jayne Greenacre, co-writer and researcher

Brian Grint, local historian

Acknowledgements

Jackie Clover, without whose inspiration and foresight this book would not have been written.

Acle Community Archive members - Robert Jermy, Lynn Kerslake, Kathy Stacey, Vivien Moore and Basil Tibbenham for their patience and support.

Clare Everitt, Picture Norfolk Administrator at the Norfolk and Norwich Millennium Library for recovering the photographs and digitalizing the collection.

Peter Freeman for the loan of his original cartes de visites.

The Ancient House Museum, Thetford for the use of the Signor Ægena cartoon.

All images courtesy of Norfolk County Council Library and Information Service except for The Crystal Palace Exhibition Catalogue, the Signor Ægena cartoon and the original cartes de visites provided by Peter Freeman. Copyright held. Original captions in italics. To view more photographs from the Finch collection, please go to www.picture.norfolk.gov.uk.

Cover photograph - W. Finch, *'Acle near the bridge. Group of men and yacht'* (Original caption).

Title page photograph - W. Finch, *'Photographic Studio'* (Original caption).
This is believed to be Arthur Finch, aged about 12 years old, with his father's barrow. On the wagon is painted 'Ægena Fynch, Veteran Photographer, Xyloidine Cottage, Acle'.

Contents

Introduction

The Norfolk village of Acle is in a prime position almost equidistant from Great Yarmouth and Norwich, with the river Bure flowing out to the coast in one direction and to the beautiful Norfolk Broads in the other. It is for this reason that the village is known as 'The Gateway to the Broads'. Acle currently has a population of about 2,500, yet it still retains some of the traditional character that would have drawn William Henry Finch there in the nineteenth century.

In 1988 a box of 148 photographs of Acle was found in the depths of Norwich Library and passed on to Brian Grint, a local historian who was researching a book on the village and who was given to understand that these were part of the Walter Rye Collection[1.]

The photographs, all dated between 1863 and 1883, were the work of Eugenia Fynch, an Acle resident. These photographs of street scenes and portraits were wonderful documented evidence of nineteenth century life in a rural Norfolk village. What made them unique was the fact they were taken twenty years before Francis Frith and P. H. Emerson documented the area, and their quality, for the time, was outstanding.

The photographs were copied and returned to the library for archiving but after the devastating fire that destroyed the library in August 1994, most of the original copies were thought to have been lost.

The Acle Community Archive Group (ACAG) was set up in 2004 as a local history group capturing and archiving historical photographs and documents from the village. The copies of the Fynch photographs belonging to Brian Grint were archived by the group and during the summer of 2010, members of ACAG set about researching the life and work of the photographer, the connection to the village and thus the origin of this remarkable photographic legacy.

---

[1] http://en.wikisource.org/wiki/The_Times/1929/Obituary/Walter_Rye

Eugenia Fynch of Acle was listed in both the 'Photographers of Great Britain and Ireland 1840-1940'[2] and the 'Whites History, Gazetteer and Directory of Norfolk, 1883'. The initial assumption was that Eugenia was a woman however, on closer inspection of the photographs that depicted the photographer's barrow, it became apparent that the name was mis-spelt. The directory references should have read 'Ægena Fynch' with the Greek spelling. Despite trawling the census, Ægena Fynch remained elusive. It was only when the Acle census of 1871 was investigated that a William Finch, Photographer was found and a connection made. Ægena was a pseudonym. It was only then that this remarkable man's story could be uncovered. Whilst censuses, birth, marriage and death certificates gave the bare bones with which to work, it was historical and local knowledge that added the flesh to the story.

Contact with Clare Everitt, Picture Norfolk Administrator at the Norfolk and Norwich Millennium Library, sparked a new search for any surviving Fynch photographs and an amazing breakthrough came when the original box of prints turned up in an unexpected part of the library. For twenty-two years the photographs had remained unrecognised and unattributed. When the box was opened and the discovery made, the excitement was overwhelming.

The story did not end there however. Spurred on by the discovery, members of ACAG decided to look deeper into the historic collections covering the Broadland area. Many unassigned photographs within the collections, stretching from Blofield and Lingwood in the west, Great Yarmouth in the east and the village of Winterton in the north, were suddenly identified as being those of Fynch as the photographic cart displaying the recognizable name was often in view.

It soon became apparent that the originals were of great quality and historical importance and that Fynch had travelled a vast distance recording the people and places of the Broadland area. In 2011 the Eugenia Fynch photographs grew to become a major collection and are now filed under the photographer's real name, William Henry Finch.

[2] Ron Cosens 2009

W. Finch '*Acle from entrance to the new road*'
'The Street' in Acle showing the original Folly Tree which sadly died of Dutch Elm Disease in the 1980s. Ægena Fynch's barrow can be seen in the centre of the picture surrounded by a group of curious children.

Chapter 1

William Henry Finch (1816-1883) of Norwich

William Henry Finch was born in Norwich, the oldest of six surviving children of parents William Henry and Ruth and lived in Waggon and Horses Lane, off Elm Hill, in the city. He was a whitesmith[3] like his father and his grandfather before him. There is some question over the actual year of William's birth. On his gravestone in Acle St Edmund's churchyard he is alleged to have been born in 1819, however there is a record of a William Henry Finch, son of William Henry and Ruth being christened at St Saviour's Church, Norwich on the 22nd December, 1816. This would be the true and accepted date.

Little was known about William's early life except for one major incident that must have shaken the whole family. William's half uncle, Francis Finch, was caught stealing copper, maybe to supplement the family business. He was convicted at the Norwich assizes on the 26th July 1834 and transported to Australia in 1835. The story was not such an unhappy one however as, when Francis got his 'ticket of leave' in 1842, he decided to remain in Australia, took a 'common law wife', had some children and became a successful and well respected blacksmith. They lived happily in Parramatta, New South Wales until his death in 1863. His life in Australia must have been a far cry from the slum areas of the Norwich Yards.

Norwich was not a good place to be for the less well off at this time. From the 16th century, with the influx of Flemish weavers and agricultural workers seeking employment within the city walls, housing was of a premium. The wealthy merchants moved from the city to avoid the overcrowded conditions and 'The Yards' developed within their gardens, orchards and courtyards and within the stable areas behind public houses and inns. Every small piece of land was utilized and developed into homes for the poorer members of society. They were crowded

---

[3] A whitesmith is a metal worker who deals in light coloured metals such as tin and pewter. They may also work on enamelled goods and cooking ware. Unlike a blacksmith, the whitesmith works on cold metals and rarely uses a forge.

and often sanitary conditions were poor. There had been two major cholera epidemics in the city in 1831 and 1848 and it was not until 1869 that the Norwich Corporation laid its first sewer[4]. Yet despite these conditions, communities developed and the yards remained home to many people until the early 20th century when purpose built social housing was introduced. It was in the Norwich Yards that the Finch family had lived and worked for generations.

On the 10th November 1839, at the age of twenty-three, William married a Thetford girl, Mary Ann Baker who was a weaver. Her father James was a tailor. At this time William had already got a taste for the exotic and possibly the desire to better himself. He changed the spelling of his middle name on his marriage certificate from Henry to the French, Henri.

In 1841 William, still working as a whitesmith, was living in Fish Yard in Norwich, with wife Mary Ann and the first of their children who also bore the family name, William Henry. Fish Yard was off what is now known as Fishergate, and was just a short stroll from Waggon and Horses Yard, across the river Wensum.

Strangely, in 1851 William was missing from the census. Wife, Mary Ann had moved again and was living in Red Lion Yard in Norwich with her three children, William, Walter and Mary Ann. Her profession was listed as a 'tailoress' and she was still registered as being married.

There are a number of possible theories for William's absence in 1851, one of them being that, like one third of the population of Britain, he may have been staying in London to visit The Great Exhibition that was held from May until October of that year. What a spectacle it would have been for an untravelled Norfolk man! For a one shilling ticket he would have been able to spend a full day marvelling at the wonderful new inventions in the fields of art, science, and manufacture from both home and abroad, and of course, one of the stars of the day was the newly invented art of photography.

---

[4] 'Victorian Norfolk', Jonathan Mardles, George Nobbs Publishing, 1981

The Crystal Palace Exhibition Illustrated Catalogue, London 1851

'In addition to its thousands of other exhibits, it incorporated the first large international exhibition of photography, exhibiting a range of materials and styles that most of the public had never before witnessed. (Terms like *photograph, positive,* and *negative* had to be explained in the catalogue.) …..The exhibition, which was visited by over 6 million people, not only increased awareness of photography in general but publicized important innovations; most notably Archer's revolutionary wet plate process.'[5]

Had he been there, William would have witnessed the new equipment and photographic processes that were being introduced. He may have looked in awe at the photographic images from photographers with exotic names, from far off countries. It would have been a revelation to his narrow Norfolk lifestyle. He would also have been inspired by the photographs of a fellow Norwich man, Joseph Cundall, the son of a draper and born in the same year as William himself. Joseph had been apprenticed to a Norwich printer but had moved to London in 1834 where his publishing and photographic career flourished. William may have witnessed this and seen photography as a pathway to a new life and career, a chance to move away from the Norwich Yards and to develop his own creative talents.

Another possible theory for William's absence from the 1851 census was that he was visiting Great Yarmouth, staying at the home of Henry Forrest, a fellow whitesmith. The visitors name on the census reads 'William Curtis, portrait painter'. Two other guests to the family home at that time were Polish hawkers.

---

[5] Reference: Answers.com/The Great Exhibition

This man was born in the right place, at the right time and on investigation of previous and following censuses, William Curtis never appears again. It was only after suspecting this connection that it was discovered William had indeed changed his profession by this time from whitesmith to painter. This was corroborated on his wife's death certificate of 1852.

Mary Ann died from dropsy from which she had been suffering for two years. She had described herself as 'Head' on the 1851 census in William's absence indicating that he had been away from the home for some time. There is no record of his being a prison inmate so it can only be assumed that he was working away. There is always the possibility that he had left Mary Ann and the children, however this is unlikely because after her death the children are found living with their father and his new wife.

Yet another theory for William's absence at this time was postulated after a digital enlargement of a photograph of William Henry's barrow revealed a small line of text reading,

'Formerly scenic and mechanical artist to Messrs. Andrew Ducrow, J. Ryan and W. Cooke & Son.'

This proffers the idea that William may have travelled with the circuses of the time painting backdrops and rides. Historical research recounts that all three of these men ran famous circuses, with strong influences from Spain and Greece. This may have coloured William's outlook and provided him with a vehicle to demonstrate the artistic ability that was so evident in the painted scenic backgrounds of his later photographic work. It cannot be definitively established that William ever worked for any of the above proprietors although it seems unlikely. Existing lists of circus staff pertaining to Cooke's have been searched and revealed nothing whilst Ducrow's circus ended in the 1840s. However the public would have known these world famous names thus enhancing Finch's reputation. An excellent advertising strategy!

The first time that William was recorded as being a 'photographic artist' was on his son, Eugene Arthur's, birth certificate in 1857. There were many events at this time that could have influenced this change of career, including the launch of the Norwich and District Photographic Society in June 1854. This was formed by some budding photographic enthusiasts, amongst them one J. R. Sawyer (1828-1889) who opened a studio in the city in 1853 and became a prominent figure in the Norwich photographic circle. The first President of the society was Thomas

Adamant Eaton (1800-1871), a silk merchant from Norwich who retired from business in 1846 to devote his time to painting and photography[6].

The Norwich and District Photographic Society was one of the first of its kind in the country. It 'existed for only seven years but during that time it had an influence on the development of photography far greater than its provincial origins merited; there are reports about its meetings in the archives of the Royal Photographic Society.'[7]

Photography was in its infancy at this stage, the official birth date being 1839 when both Louis Jacques Mandé Daguerre (1787-1851) and William Henry Fox Talbot (1800-1877) independently announced their discoveries to the world. Both the daguerreotype and the calotype methods of photography flourished and were soon to take over in popularity from the traditional art of painting. In these early days of photography equipment was expensive and the scientific knowledge exclusive to the elite. It was certainly not a poor man's hobby. The skill of the photographer soon found its way to Norwich and the first studio advertising 'Patent Life-like Likenesses Taken by the Action of Light in a few seconds', opened in St Andrew's Broad Street in 1843.[8]

In 1856 the Norwich Photographic Society organized an exhibition of photographic work at St Andrew's Hall. It was a huge and very influential event running for four months and included 394 exhibits from around the country. The exhibitors' list[9] showed the work of such photographers as Frederick Scott Archer (1813-1857), the originator of the collodion wet plate, Roger Fenton (1819-1869), known mostly for his later work as the first war photographer in the Crimea, and Joseph Cundall, local man, once again.

With humble beginnings from the Norwich Yards, it was assumed that William would not have attended the Norwich Society meetings, predominantly frequented by professional men. However it was later discovered that his daughter Mary Ann Finch married Charles Freeman, the nephew of William Philip Barnes Freeman,

---

[6] Ian Sumner 'Encyclopaedia of Nineteenth Century Photography, Vol 1'
[7] Norwich and District Photographic Society –
[8] 'When Found Make A Note' David D Button LRPS, Norwich and District Photographic Society, 2003 ISBN 0-9545541-0-8
[9] De Montfort University, Leicester.
    www.peib.dmu.ac.uk/itemexhibition.php?. . . exhibitionTitle=1856%2C+Norwich%2C+Photographic

painter and photographer, who hosted the first ever Norwich meeting. In amongst a collection of personal letters held at the Norfolk Records Office, an indirect mention of Mary Ann was found in a correspondence to Mrs. Freeman describing Charles' marriage as 'a queer match'. Thus it is known that William Henry did have tenuous connections with at least one member of the Norwich Photographic Society.

Like anybody with the slightest interest in photography, William Henry would have undoubtedly attended the 1856 exhibition. It would have been a very influential and important event for both the city of Norwich and the history of photography, attracting huge crowds who, for the first time ever, could see photographs from abroad as well as at home. With the invention of the wet collodion process photographic equipment became more portable and travel photography had arrived in earnest.

The only knowledge of the family's whereabouts and activities during this time comes from registration records. On Eugene Arthur's birth certificate the mother, Mary Ann Finch formerly Hamling (sic) lived at the Beach in Lowestoft, an area of fisherman's cottages, smokehouses and net yards. Despite investigations, it remains a mystery as to why Arthur was born in Lowestoft as all other records pertaining to the family's whereabouts at this time point to the family living in Norwich.

Mary Ann Hambling was born in Norwich in 1831 thus making her some fifteen years William's junior. Intensive research has so far failed to uncover a marriage certificate for this match. This does not rule out the possibility that Mary Ann had previously married and would therefore have been registered under a different surname.

In 1859 their last child was born, a daughter called Ruth Rachel, named after William Henry's mother. Interestingly, on her birth certificate the father's occupation was listed as a 'painter' rather than as a 'photographic artist' demonstrating William's artistic versatility. On the 1861 census William Henry and Mary Ann Finch lived in Sparkes Yard off Waggon and Horses Lane in Norwich, along with eldest son William, 21, now assistant to his father, Walter, 18, Arthur (Eugene), 4 and baby Ruth, the younger two being the children of the second wife. His daughter Mary Ann, aged 14, lived with her grandparents just a few doors away. The next record of the Finches appears in the 1871 census when William and his family are linked to Acle for the first time.

W. Finch '*Norwich Cow Tower*'. We suspect that this is one of the few surviving and identified Finch photographs taken in Norwich before his move to Acle, thus dating it to the late 1850s or early 1860s.

Chapter 2

Ægena Fynch of Acle

The collection contains photographs of Acle, accredited to W. Finch, that are dated 1863. It has been assumed therefore that the family moved to the village at about this time, although no definitive information has been found to corroborate this. It would have been an opportune time to relocate from the overcrowded and unhygienic conditions of the Yards. As late as 1886 the Medical Officer of Health reported that the infant mortality rate in Norwich was more than one in five, and record epidemics of typhoid and diphtheria were evident in the city. It would have been a great career move for William as by this time there were a number of photographic studios popping up all over Norwich. Being in Acle put William in a unique position as he would have monopolized the market with the local gentry who all wanted their families and their homes captured for posterity.

At this time in history Acle, with a population of just 850, was experiencing a boom period. In 1848 it famously held the annual flower show, which included animals and agricultural equipment and was a forerunner of the Royal Norfolk Show. It was attended by a magnificent crowd of over 6,000 people! The New Road from Acle to Great Yarmouth had been opened in 1831 with coaches running four times a day from Norwich, thus making Acle an ideal stopping off point being midway between the city and the town. In 1844 the railway arrived in nearby Reedham, taking passengers from Norwich to Great Yarmouth in relative comfort and in no time at all. A school had opened by 1859 and to William the expanding market town of Acle would have been an area of prosperity and the ideal place to set up his new business.

W. Finch, *'Acle School'*. A grant was made to the Rector and church wardens for the building of a school and signed by Lord Calthorpe in 1859.

The rented cottage that they moved to belonged to the Calthorpe Manor and had a yard fronting Old Road in Acle. The large yard would have been very important for the outdoor production of photographic prints which at that time were developed by the power of the sun and not in a darkroom. Some of the Finch photographs in the collection are taken from the cottage looking across to the blacksmith's shop opposite. There is also a view taken from the upper window of the cottage looking up the road at the passers-by. Sadly, all that remains today of the Finch family home is a part of the brick boundary wall.

W. Finch, *'Acle Blacksmith's Shop and Mrs Hinchcliffe's house'*. A view from the window of Xyloidine Cottage.

In the 1850s photography had had major breakthroughs. A number of new processes had been presented with the most popular being the wet collodion process, first published by Frederick Scott Archer in 1851. We know that William used this process as he left us a very big clue. His new address was 'Xyloidine Cottage', xyloidine, or gun cotton being a major component of the photographic process. Interestingly, the cottage kept its unusual name until it was demolished in the 1980s.

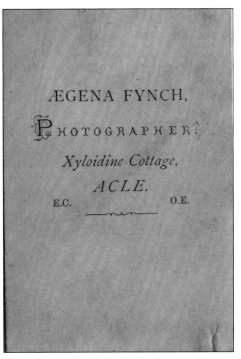

ÆGENA FYNCH,

PHOTOGRAPHER,

Xyloidine Cottage,

ACLE.

E.C.   O.E.

The back of one of Ægena Fynch's photographs dated July 11 1881

The wet collodion process involved coating a glass plate with collodion, a solution of gun cotton in ethyl alcohol and ethyl ether. It was the dissolved gun cotton that was known as xyloidine. Once tacky, the plate was further sensitised with silver nitrate solution and the picture was exposed whilst still moist. The plate was developed immediately after exposure with pyrogallic acid or ferrous sulphate and then fixed with hyposulphite of soda or potassium cyanide. It was a messy and dangerous process, with elements needing to be carried out in situ. The concentration of ether vapour led to explosions in badly ventilated darkrooms and the process became known as the 'Black Art' due to the skin staining properties of the silver nitrate.

Unfortunately its inventor, Frederick Scott Archer, did not patent the wet collodion process and sadly died in poverty just six years after publishing his discovery. It was thanks to him though, along with new improvements to cameras making them smaller and cheaper to manufacture, that photography became more widely available. The practice of the art was now accessible for the man on the street and photographic studios flourished throughout the country. Wealthier photographers would have had a well ventilated darkroom attached to their studios that would be specially adapted for the purpose of mixing chemicals and coating plates. The poorer, itinerant photographers, such as William, would have had a simple barrow that could be taken to locations for the purpose of photographing landscapes and informal portraiture. The photographers would cover their heads with a dark cloth whilst coating and developing the plates, thus breathing in all the toxic chemical fumes and making them prone to respiratory diseases.

A closer look at the only recognised photograph of William himself shows that he has two such barrows, one large and one small. Beautifully inscribed on the side of his barrow in his sign writer's hand are the words 'Ægena Fynch, Veteran Photographer, Xyloidine Cottage, Acle'.

W. Finch, '*Acle Photographers dark room after being damaged'.* This is the only recognised photograph of William Henry Finch. He is surveying the damage done to his barrow which has tilted, causing the door to open and bottles and apparatus to fall out. He is showing shock and horror in his pose.

Nobody knows why William adopted the unusual work name 'Ægena Fynch'. With many new photographic businesses starting up, he obviously needed to impress his new audience and perhaps he thought the exotic name 'Ægena' would be a good marketing ploy to launch his new career. As the itinerant photographer often found work with fairgrounds and circuses, it may have been that the Greek influence came from the theatrical circus performances of the time or simply the colourful and unusual names of the travelling circus folk. Whatever the reason, the profession of a roving photographic artist must have seemed quite exotic to the Broadland residents.

William's photographic work spanned almost three decades during a time when photography had developed from a privileged and extraordinary process to a popular and affordable art form. The known collection of William Finch's work shows him to have been a prolific photographer who not only capitalized on the gentry's need for immortalization but also provided a social commentary of the common man. In an era when thousands of Norfolk folk never travelled more than ten miles from their native village, William Finch may well have been considered a most unusual man.

William died on the 15th March 1883 at the age of sixty-five from 'Paralysis', an earlier name for a stroke, and 'Bronchitis'. Sadly, the Acle business died along with its owner. After William's death Mary Ann remained in Acle moving from Xyloidine Cottage to Moulton Road, and then to Middlesex Terrace. On both the 1891 and the 1901 census, she was living with one of her grandchildren. She died in 1910 in the Lingwood Workhouse at the age of seventy-eight years, having no family left locally to support her. She was buried along with William Henry in the Acle St Edmund's churchyard.

W. Finch, *'Baker's Shop and flour wagon'*. This shot was taken from outside Xyloidine Cottag and is wrongly captioned, as the bakers shop was in fact further down the road. The sign on the wagon reads, 'J and J Colman, Carrow'.

Chapter 3

William Henry Finch, Junior (1840-1889)

A photograph from 1869 bears the label 'Sig. Ægena's Sixpenny Carte de Visite, Magdalen Gates, Norwich'. You would be mistaken in thinking that this was the work of William Henry Finch from Acle. It is in fact a photograph taken by his eldest son, also William Henry. His father's penchant for an exotic business name had obviously rubbed off on his son. The Finch photographic empire was beginning to spread.

William Henry (Jnr) was born on 17th February 1840 and christened a month later at St George, Tombland, Norwich. In 1861, at the age of 21, he was working as an assistant to his photographer father and living with the family in Sparkes Yard, Waggon and Horses Lane. By 1871 William was lodging at 'The Saracen's Head' in Mount Street, Diss with a woman called Charlotte Ægena and they were both listed as being married. Interestingly he named his birth place as being 'London', yet it is known from official records that this was not the case.

Charlotte Ægena, nee Sly, was born in Bawdeswell, Norfolk to parents John and Ann. On 11th March 1838 she was baptized at the parish church of All Saints. On the 1841 census John's occupation was listed as a 'baker' and the Sly family, along with a number of 'orphans' and 'paupers' were listed as living on the Street in Bawdeswell. Charlotte, interestingly, was named as an 'inmate'. From subsequent census returns it seems that the Sly family was travelling fairground folk, living in tents and caravans and selling confectionery for a living. This all added to the picture that was being built of the Finch family who, working as itinerant photographers, may well have travelled with the same fairground people and thus have adopted the desire for the exotic. As an artist and painter, William Henry (Snr) may well have decorated the fairground rides and produced the signage for advertising the travelling fair. His talent for sign-writing is evident in the decoration of his own barrow. It may well have been, whilst working with his father at the fair, that William Henry (Jnr) met Charlotte Sly. One of the photographs in this collection is captioned 'Gipsies in Pyebush Lane, Acle'. It has been speculated that these are the faces of the Finch/Sly families as they took a stroll in their Sunday best.

W. Finch, '*Acle Pye Bush Lane. Gypsy party'*. It is commonly known that travellers frequented Pye Bush Lane yet we suspect by the elegant dress, that these may not be gipsies. Note the kettle on the right. It is hanging from what appears to be a photographic tripod.

In 1881 Sig. Henri and Charlotte Ægena lived at 11 White Hart Street, Thetford as a married couple, however, it was not until 1884 that William actually made an 'honest woman' of Charlotte and they finally wed in Thetford. He was forty four and she was forty six years of age. Their marriage certificate provided evidence that Sig. Henri Ægena was indeed William Henri Finch, the man from the Norwich Yards and not the London born cosmopolitan he had earlier purported to be. William and Charlotte had been living together as husband and wife for over thirteen years at this stage, which begs the question, why did they finally decide to wed?

There is a wonderful photograph of the property in White Hart Street displaying signs for, 'Sig. Ægena Artist' and home of the, 'Thetford Institute of Photography'. Every inch of window space displays examples of Signor Henri's work and a coat of arms below a wall mounted camera, advertises his regal status. He sold himself as a carver and gilder, a general writer, a sign painter, optician, sculptor, decorator, picture framer and even a royal wizard, under the patronage of his Royal Highness the Prince of Wales. William Henri (Jnr) certainly seemed to be moving up in the world as the back of his carte de visites now grandly boasted, 'From the Royal Italian Studio of H. Ægena Artist & Photographer'. Equally on the back of one of his remaining portraits was a seemingly morbid advertisement for, 'Small or imperfect portraits of deceased or absent friends copied and finished in any style, up to life size. 100 various views of Thetford to select from for 6d each.'

The back of one of Sig. Ægena's portraits

Sig. Henri Ægena, shop front, 11 White Hart Street, Thetford

William, like his father, was also an artist and some of his cartoons satirizing the candidates in the Thetford local elections remain at the town's Ancient House Museum. They are a particularly elaborate commentary on the social and political life at that time and show that William Henri was an intelligent and astute man.

A cartoon signed H. Ægena 1875 © The Ancient House Museum, Thetford

William may have picked up his love of all things Italian from his early years in the Norwich Yards where a thriving Italian community had been growing for some years. He may also have been in competition with his contemporary, John Payne Jennings, who was famed for his photographs of the Norfolk Broads. Payne Jennings was an educated man and used an Italian motto on the back of his early carte de visites. It read, 'Il buon tempo verra', meaning, 'The good times will come', and they certainly did for Payne Jennings, as he became a sought after photographer and received a number of commissions, the most famous being with the railway companies. He also published a number of photographic books. 'Sun Pictures of the Norfolk Broads'[10] contained one hundred of his photographs, including 'Wherries at Acle Bridge' and 'The Angel Inn, Acle Bridge' dated circa 1880, so their paths may well have crossed. Sadly our Finch photographers were never to receive such notoriety.

---

[10] Published by Jarrolds, Norwich 1891

With the popularization of photography, the Sixpenny Portrait was a must for every home. What a thrill to have seen your own image for the first time, a previous luxury only known by those who could afford to sit for a portrait painter. Most sixpenny portraits or 'cartes de visites' were mounted on a simple card backing but wealthier clients had their pictures displayed in elaborate papier maché or metal casings. Everybody at this time wanted to have their image immortalized and photographic studios were opening up all over the country. Albumen printing

paper, as discovered by Blanquart-Evrard in 1850, was in such high demand that the first battery chicken farm was opened in order to provide the egg whites that formed the basis for the paper's coating.

Little more is known about the life and career of William Henri (Jun). Sadly Signor Henri Ægena, as he like to be called, died in 1889. He was just forty-nine years old. He and Charlotte had been married just five years but had been in a working partnership for over eighteen. They did not have any children, but the couple must have done very well for themselves as, after William's death, Charlotte is found living in Mountergate Street, Norwich as a 'Lodging

Sig Henri Ægena. A studio portrait, sitter unknown. Note the elaborately painted backdrop.

House Keeper'. On the 1911 census Charlotte Ægena Finch, widow, aged seventy three, was living alone in a four roomed house on the Dereham Road in Norwich. Despite her comfortable surroundings she was still working from home as a 'Phunologist (sic) and Palmist', in other words, a fortune teller. She had gone back to her fairground roots - you can take the woman out of the fairground, but you can't take the fairground out of the woman. Although Charlotte had left the fairground life over four decades earlier, it was obviously a part of her that she never forgot. It appeared that she, like her husband, would have been a very enigmatic character.

Mr Finch (Sig Henri Ægena) 1879. *'Thetford Observatory – Government Survey'*

Chapter 4

Walter Juan Finch (1843-1888)

The Finch photographic empire continued to spread with William Henry's second son, Walter Juan who was soon to follow in his father's and older brother's footsteps. He was born in 1843, in Waggon and Horses Lane, Norwich and was named after William Henry's younger brother. Once again, the family's fascination for exotic names is evident.

Walter married Sarah Ann Precious in 1865 and by the age of twenty-eight, had set up in business as a photographer in Red Lion Street, Aylsham. It is suspected that the picture below, taken in Bank Street, Aylsham, is of Sarah Ann with the eldest of their nine children, Rosa May, Walter Juan and Harry Juan. The photograph would have been taken before 1873 as, sadly, Harry Juan died in that year. As well as the Red Lion Street studio, Walter Juan worked at several other premises including his two Norwich studios, at 39, Prince of Wales Road, and then at 32, St Giles Street.

W. J. Finch, *'Bank Street, Aylsham'*

Walter is listed by Ron Cosens in; 'Photographers of Great Britain & Ireland 1840-1940' as having a portable studio in Aylsham. There are a few photographs taken on Cromer Beach that are credited to Walter J. Finch, dated August, 1876. The early photographers' website offers an insight as to why Walter may have been in Cromer at this time. 'If this refers to the Aylsham photographer, the picture may be the result of summer resort work with portable tintype equipment. It would not have been necessary to return to the studio to process the picture'.[11]

W. J. Finch, *'Cromer Sands Donkeys'*. The original Cromer Pier can be seen in the background.

Like his father and brother before him, Walter Juan also displayed artistic talents, as advertised on the back of his carte de visites, 'Pictures of every description copied, enlarged, reduced and finished in oil, water or crayon to order.'

[11] http://www.cartedevisite.co.uk/about-2/ron-cosens

The back of one of Walter Juan's portraits.

Walter was hand tinting black and white photographs at this stage as the advent of colour photography was still a long way off. Experiments in colouring photographs had been taking place since the 1850s and in 1868 Louis Ducon du Hauron patented a colour process using three colour filtered negatives. These required hours of exposure in the camera however, making the process impractical. The first commercial colour process, the Autochrome invented by the Lumiere Brothers. It was not available until 1907, so hand colouring was still very much in vogue during Walter Juan's lifetime.

In a style similar to his father and brother, Walter Juan photographed local street scenes, churches, rectories, large houses and some portraits. There is one striking group portrait of the 'Aylsham Volunteers', probably taken while the weekend soldiers were relaxing on their annual camp. With bottles of drink in hand, they were most certainly not prepared for fighting.

In the late 1880's the surviving Finch brothers would have been well aware of the most famous of Norfolk photographers, Dr Peter Henry Emerson. Emerson's first portfolio of photographs, published in 1886, was entitled 'Life and Landscape on the Norfolk Broads', and consisted of 40 platinum prints. In the same year he gave a passionate lecture to a packed audience at the Priory Hall, Great Yarmouth promoting photography as a pictorial art,

'By photography, can be expressed more truthfully and beautifully the beauties of nature than by any other black and white process – the drawing of the lens is unequalled, the tomes of the platinotype are perfect.'

W. J. Finch, '*Aylsham Group of Volunteers*'.

Emerson, who was born in Cuba, lived in Southwold, Suffolk at this time. He took beautifully composed photographs in natural settings portraying Norfolk as a tranquil idyll. His work was described by Peter Turner and Richard Wood as 'direct and honest, albeit in rather a romantic fashion'[12]. Although beautiful in their own right, Emerson's photographs look posed and staid and seem to lack the realities of Victorian life that are evident in the Finch collection.

In 1886 Walter Juan's wife, Sarah Ann, died after the birth of their ninth child, Charles Sydney. She was just thirty-nine years of age. On the death certificate the causes are listed as chronic Bright's disease (kidney disease), diabetes and parturition phlegmasia (phlebitis after childbirth). Walter Juan was present at her death.

---

[12] P. H. Emerson: Photographer of Norfolk/Peter Turner and Richard Wood. Boston: D. R. Godine, [1974]

By this time the family was living in The Thoroughfare, Harleston where Walter Juan was recorded as having a studio. He lived here with his seven surviving children, Rosa May, Walter Juan (Jnr), Gertrude Eva, Edith, Harry William, William Henry and baby, Charles Sydney. It probably fell on Rosa May, now aged twenty-one to look after her smaller siblings.

Sadly, Walter Juan did not live for long to enjoy his children. Just two years after Sarah Ann's death, on 28th February 1888, he died at the age of forty-five years. The cause of death was listed as 'cardiac valvular disease, 1 year and Bright's disease, 7 months'. Rosa May was present at his death. Both he and Sarah are buried in St Mary's churchyard in Redenhall, Norfolk .

Walter Juan made a comfortable living from his photographic career leaving a personal estate of £370 11s 11d. This, along with the guardianship of his six surviving children, went to his sister Mary Ann, now Freeman, named as the 'only next of kin'. Sadly, just three months after the death of her father, Gertrude Eva was placed in Muller's orphanage in Barton Regis, Gloucestershire. Her two brothers, William Henry and Charles Sydney were to join her there some six months later and it was here that Gertrude and Charles both died. Of all of Walter Juan's nine children, it is believed that only four survived to adulthood.

Mary Ann and husband Charles Freeman, a Norwich born cabinet maker and upholsterer, had moved to Weymouth shortly after the Norfolk business had been declared bankrupt. In the 1891 census, they lived with their six children and employed a general servant. It seemed that in the preceding years and shortly after the inheritance from his brother-in-law, Charles gained status with Masonic connections and a number of successful businesses, namely upholsterer, auditor, cabinetmaker, undertaker, furniture remover, estate agent and public recognition as a magistrate. One can only speculate at the circumstances that led to Walter Juan's children being committed to and dying in an orphanage over 100 miles away from their home.

W. J. Finch. *'Blickling Hall Library Interior'*. A rare interior shot with natural lighting from windows, illuminating intricate detail of ceiling, walls and book shelves.

Chapter 5

Eugene Arthur Finch (1857–1883)

William Henry's third son, known as Arthur, was born to his second wife, Mary Ann Hamling (sic), at the Beach community in Lowestoft in 1857. Little is known about his life, yet we have a very good idea of what he looked like. By the time William Henry's photographic business was established in Acle, the older brothers were building careers for themselves. It was left for the youngest son, Arthur to assist his father as he walked miles pushing the photographic barrow from village to village. From Lingwood in the south-west, to Winterton on Sea in the north-east, we have evidence of William Henry's work. The themes are the same in each village; the church, the rectory, any large halls, farms or houses along with their owners sitting on the lawn, public houses, school houses, the blacksmith's shop and any other business worth its note. While the collection contains many portraits of the clergy and other local dignitaries, Finch's most enigmatic work often features the ordinary man on the street or a group of local children attracted by this strange fellow and his magical art.

Through the work of the father we can watch Arthur growing up as he appears, sometimes unknowingly, in his father's photographs. From Braydeston, where Arthur is perched on a gate, to the shot of 'Beighton Old Stepping Stone' where we get a clear picture of Arthur aged about thirteen years old. It was Arthur's appearance in Kitty Witches Row in Great Yarmouth that helped in the

identification of the few Great Yarmouth photographs attributed to William Finch. It appears that when William senior felt the picture lacked a clear focal point then Arthur was often introduced to add interest.

'Bradeston Hills. Distant view of Blofield Church'

33

'Beighton – old stepping stone'

This is a beautiful portrait of Arthur Finch sitting on the old stone that was used for mounting horses. In the background is his father's photographic barrow. The stone is dated 1668 but the significance of this date is unknown. The stone still stands on what is known as Stone Corner.

'Row 95. Kitty Witches Row, looking North'. Arthur can be seen looking into a doorway in the famous Kitty Witches Row in Great Yarmouth.

Further to these pictorial images, a letter dated September 11th 1877 from one John D Smith to his father, was discovered in the Norfolk library archive. It was sent from the Queen's Head, Acle where Mr. Smith was staying as a guest. The letter tells of Mr. Smith's day trip to St Benet's Abbey with Arthur and their quest to photograph the scenic abbey ruins that stand beside the River Bure. The letter tells of an adventurous day sailing to the site, erecting the tent which they used for processing, setting up the camera in deep mud and

'…While we were preparing the plate for another view of the archway, three gentlemen from a yacht came up in a boat. We asked them to stand in the view and they were so pleased with the result, that they asked us if we could take them in their yacht. We said that we were only amateurs… but we would do our best.'

Arthur Finch and J. D. Smith. *St Benet's Abbey'*.

Smith's letter provides a unique insight into the life and work of an itinerant photographer at this time, demonstrating the thought and effort involved in obtaining just a few finished photographic plates. The letter also gives a small glimpse of William Henry Finch himself.

'…We commenced trudging home with our packs on our backs. We met poor Mr. Finch just past the Hermitage, he was in great trouble, having just seen a vision of Arthur & I struggling to get there in the water……When we showed him the pictures, he was very pleased with our day's work & said they could not have been better. Arthur says he had never spent a happier day. I am sure I never did.'

Arthur was being modest when he told the yachtsmen that he was a mere amateur. He had spent his entire life assisting his father and had by now broken away and started out on his own. It was inevitable that Arthur would follow in his father's and brothers' footsteps. By 1881 Arthur is found living at 4 High Street, Southwold with his wife Elizabeth Jane, nee Tennant and their two children, William James, aged two and two day old George Arthur. Like his father and brother before him, Arthur had also adopted the family pseudonym, and had become Arthur Ægena Finch. This may have been a corruption of his birth name, Eugene. Having married in 1876 in the Blything registration district Suffolk, they had settled in Southwold with Elizabeth's widowed aunt, Eliza Court. Eliza was also listed as a photographer and watchmaker, the profession of her deceased husband, James.

William Henry (Jnr) had set up business in south Norfolk, Walter Juan had moved to the north of the county and now Arthur was working in Southwold in the east and thus branching into Suffolk. With father William Henry centralized in Acle, the Finch family appeared to be working the entire region.

There are few photographs presently attributed to Arthur, and none that are from his time in Southwold. Sadly his photographic career was very short lived as, on 21st October 1883 he died from 'Phthisis Pulmonalis', otherwise known as consumption or tuberculosis. He was only twenty-six years old. His mother was at his bedside when he died, just as she had been six months earlier, at the death of her husband, William Henry. Is it just a coincidence that all the male members of the family, all photographers, died at such an early age? Although William Henry (Snr) made it to the ripe old age of sixty-five, William Henri was forty-nine, Walter Juan was forty-five and Arthur was just twenty-six. William Henry (Snr) came to photography quite late in his life, William Henri (Jnr) and Walter Juan were both in their teens, but Arthur was weaned on photography, breathing in those noxious gases from his earliest days. Could this indicate a correlation between exposure to the toxic chemicals and the life expectancy of the itinerant, Victorian photographer?

Chapter 6

The Origins of the Collection

During the course of research at the Norwich Library some later photographs credited to both W. Finch and J.D. Smith were unearthed. This led to speculation that William Henry may have been training Mr. Smith in the photographic art. It was, of course, J.D. Smith who was the author of the letter referring to the expedition to St Benet's Abbey. At the time, the significance of the J.D. Smith connection was unknown but it later proved to be the first clue to the origins of the collection. Research identified J.D. Smith as one John Daniel Smith from London, the son of John Smith, a wealthy importer with the East India Company. John Smith (Snr) was born in Beighton, Norfolk around 1816, Beighton being just two miles from Acle. Sadly both father and son died in Willesden in 1894 within a few months of each other.

The connection emerged whilst reading 'Victorian and Edwardian Norfolk from Old Photographs' by Philip Hepworth[13] which attributed a known Finch photograph to the J. Smith Collection. Later in the text it revealed that Walter Rye, a well known Norfolk antiquarian, had purchased over 7,000 images from the London sourced J. Smith Collection in 1896. Rye donated this purchase in its entirety to the Norwich library ten years later. The discovery of the personal letter addressed to 'Dear Papa' seemed to indicate that the J. Smith of Walter Rye's donation was in fact John Smith (Snr). He would most certainly have had the wealth to accumulate a vast collection of paintings, photographs and etchings of Norfolk as, perhaps, a reminder of his roots.

The true relationship between W.H. Finch and John Smith can only be surmised. Perhaps with his siblings still residing in Acle, John Smith may well have become acquainted with William Henry during one of his family visits. Keen to have photographic images of his birth county, it might have been possible that John funded William's enterprise, and in return William tutored his son in this new art form.

---

[13] Victorian and Edwardian Norfolk from Old Photographs, Philip Hepworth, London, B. T. Batsford, 1974

J. D. Smith. *'Priory Wall South Side Sep 1880'.* This is one of the better J D Smith prints from Great Yarmouth. Except for the St Benet's Abbey photographs, the only other J D Smith photographs in the library collection were taken in Great Yarmouth on this date. The quality was not as good as Finch's, as can be seen by the uneven coating of the glass plate negative at the bottom, another reason for believing that he was a trainee in the photographic art.

Postscript

It appeared that all the pieces of the puzzle that was 'Eugenia Fynch' had finally fitted together to complete its own colourful tableau. William Finch's eldest daughter, Mary Ann settled in Weymouth and lived a comfortable life. Youngest daughter Ruth Rachel married a John Mann and moved to Ireland. With all the male members of the family having died and the daughters living away, Mary Ann was left alone. The sole survivor of William Finch's family in Norfolk, she eventually died in the Blofield Union, Lingwood Workhouse. What became of the remaining grandchildren is not known and an advertisement in the local Norwich paper for any family members unfortunately revealed nothing. Had it not been for the combined curiosity of the Acle Community Archive Group and Clare Everitt from Picture Norfolk, then the Finch family of photographers and their remarkable contribution to the history of photography and the social documentation of nineteenth century Norfolk life, may have remained lost forever. William Henry Finch's photographic legacy may still have lain in the archives of the Norwich library, unacknowledged. At long last, 'Norfolk's unknown photographers' have been rediscovered and their story told.

A portfolio of William Henry Finch Photographs

The captions in the italics are those that are written on the original photographs.

Acle

'Acle Bridge East Side' (Names illegible). Two wild fowlers, one with a dead duck in his hand, standing in front of Acle three arch bridge that was built in 1831.

'Acle Bridge, South. Load of furniture'.
A lovely shot of a family moving house with all of their worldly goods on a wagon. This is looking North across the bridge.

'Fair time'
It is believed that this photograph is taken next to Monies Farm on the Reedham Road where the fairground used to visit on mid summer's day. This is close to the meadow where the Acle Show was regularly held.

43

'Acle Old Barn on way to New Road used as a theatre 40 years ago'.
The signs read, 'Samwells Theatre and Circus from London' 'Tumble Company and Horse Riders' and 'Box Office'

These two images are unique in the Finch collection. Whilst the top photograph was taken at the same time as the one below, it has been altered to give a representation of the Old Barn when used as a theatre forty years previously.

'Acle Old Barn on way to New Road'

'Acle Kings Head Group'
A women's brass band with an audience outside the public house that is still popular today.

'Acle Bowling Green Queens Head Hotel'
A photograph of the all male bowling team, with the children who would have been used to wipe the bowls clean. The bowling green existed behind the present day Kings Head car park. Looking closely at the characters in this photograph, the game of bowls seemed to cross all class divides.

'Acle Green looking from entrance to Yarmouth Road'
Calthorpe Cottages, named after the Lord of the Manor in the seventeenth century. The Calthorpes owned the land that Xyloidine Cottage stood on.

'Acle Bakers Shop and Mr A Squires House'
A view towards the shop advertising 'Miller, Baker and Confectioner, Grocer & Tea Dealer'. Xyloidine Cottage stood behind this shop. To the left is Mr Squire's house, regarded as the village Manor House.

'Acle 2 shops'

George Rix's General Store, with possibly the proprietor posing in the doorway. Hanging in the window are numerous pairs of socks, alternating in plain and stripes. The sign reads, 'Appointed Agent for Page Woodcocks Wind Pills in 1/1½ and 2/9 boxes and Henry's Nervine for Toothache in 1/1½ and 2/9 bottles.' This shop is now the Co-operative supermarket.

'Acle Drapers Shop'

'Grocer J. Barwood, Draper'. The Barwood family moved from Fleggburgh where Mr Barwood had been a marsh farmer of 25 acres. His wife Sophia was born in Acle. Mr Barwood was 73 on the 1881 census which was about the time that this photograph was taken

'Acle entrance to Damgate'
Jonathan Mardle in 'Victorian Norfolk' (George Nobbs Publishing, 1981) suggested that this might be a wedding party because the ivy clad building on the right was used as a chapel at this time.

'Acle Damgate, Villagers at Damgate'
A group of villagers outside some newly thatched cottages. The well that supplies fresh water can be seen in the garden behind the group.

'Acle Old Workhouse. Back view'
This photograph is wrongly captioned as the old workhouse which actually stood at the top of, what is now, New Close was destroyed by fire in1834. This is an identical building which still stands next to the New Road and is called 'The Gables'.

'Acle Model Farm 1863 Saturday afternoon'

This is a Fowler ploughing engine that was owned by contractor Alfred Watson from Thorpe, Norwich. In the early 1860s steam ploughing was introduced by John Fowler who had won the competition for its invention in 1858. In June of 1863 the Norfolk Agricultural Society held their annual show of stock and implements at Great Yarmouth. It seems that the ploughing demonstration was held at Acle at the same time. Model Farm was next to Xyloidine Cottage in Acle. Note the manipulated sky with cloud.

'Acle. Portrait of Mr William Squire and Mr (illegible)'
Mr Squire was the owner of the farm on Reedham Road. We believe that this shot was taken on the west side of the hill, now Wright's Farm. The Squire family were local farmers and landowners.

'Acle, Mr J Squire's Prize Ox'
This is a record of his prize ox, standing outside Xyloidine Cottage with the Blacksmith's shop in the background. Mr John Squire was the owner of Fishley Hall Farm. In 1871 the farm was recorded as being 380 acres and employing 13 men and 5 boys. In 1881 the farm had grown to 520 acres, employing just 12 men and 8 boys.

'Mr William Squire's House, Acle'
A panoramic shot which is an unusual format for William Henry Finch. This is now Monies Farm on the Reedham Road

se was recently restored and the pond on the right still looks the same today.

' Acle. Mr and Mrs Boardman'.
This is a picture of George Boardman and his wife Elizabeth, nee Shingles. Mr Boardman died in 1876 and Elizabeth passed away the following year, which dates the photograph to pre 1876. Mr Boardman was a school master in the day school, the school for the poor. A very Dickensian looking couple, straight out of Oliver Twist.

' *Mr Robert Russell, Acle* '

A lovely close-up portrait, beautifully posed in front of a window of geraniums. Mr Russell, the village blacksmith, is shown in his work clothes. It was unusual for Finch to take close-up photographs, in fact this is the only head and shoulders shot in this collection. This photograph was taken before July 1876 as Mr Russell's death is registered in June quarter of that year, aged 72.

'Acle New Road during flood 1878'
1878 was the severest winter for many years. Flooding in November covered the marshes with ice for several weeks and the bad weather continued for seven months. This photograph records the flooding of the New Road, thus cutting off access to Great Yarmouth.

'Acle, Causeway to bridge, Finch'
A nicely composed portrait of a man leaning on the fence with the river in the background. A wherry can be seen sailing on the horizon.

'Acle Mill & Steam Mill'

This photograph shows the tower mill and steam mill on this site, which also included a bakery and cucumber house. Note that smoke has been added to the glass plate at a later stage. This was a common practice as collodion did not record the colour blue very effectively. A mill had been recorded on the site since 1633. By 1836 the post mill had been replaced by a tower mill with the steam element being a later addition. The mill disappeared from the landscape in the early 20th century after a severe October storm in 1904. This caused the head of the mill to lurch forward, making the mill unusable.

'North Porch, Acle Church'.

The North Porch was added to Acle church in 1494. This thatched and flint building has changed very little since this photograph was taken. The grave stone of William and Mary Ann Finch may be found to the west of this porch.

Beighton

'Beighton. Old Farm, near Moulton'
Two families posing in front of the farm house. The distance between the two groups implies that they are not closely related and the difference in clothing suggests that they may be employer and employee.

'Beighton, Blacksmiths Shop'
The wheel and shadow of William Finch's barrow can be seen on the right of the picture.

'Beighton – view from the church. The site of ancient battle.'
This image is not very interesting photographically yet shows the old method of muck spreading in the fields and, as the title suggests, is the site of an ancient battle. Sadly, there is no local knowledge of this event.

Billockby

'Billockby – Sheep in Mr Ashford's farm'
This is a typical William Finch record of the working man. The movement of the sheep shows a reasonably long exposure time.

Blofield

'Blofield Paddon Mill dam with Water Cart & Butchers do' (sic)
The water cart and the butcher's wagon meeting face to face on the bridge. Paddon Mill should read 'Pedham Mill' and is located near Hemblington.

'Blofield Grocers Shop'
The shop of William Fisher, listed as 'Grocer, Draper, Painter, Plumber, & Glazier'. Born in Wymondham and married to Frances, Mr Fisher was in his seventies when this photograph was taken. The shop was in Turnpike Road, Blofield.

'Blofield. Old Farm near Paddon Mill Dam'
Another of William Finch's group shots with the farmer and his workers holding the tools of their trade and posing in front of the farm house.

'Blofield Rectory'
In contrast to the informality of the previous image, is the very formal photograph of the Rector, Thomas Smith Turnbull, and his family posing in front of the Rectory.

'Blofield Old School'
Another group school shot. The school master is posing with a globe in his hands, whilst the children are holding their chalk and slates.

Brundall

'Brundall, Ram Inn'

An idyllic country pub scene with Arthur, William's son, standing in the foreground. Arthur is in his late teens or early twenties. The name John Harper is above the pub door.

Burlingham

'St Peter Little Burlingham Church SE. Under restoration 1874'
This is a wonderful historic record of the church restoration. It was obviously a 'cowboy job' as the whole tower collapsed just thirty years later, in 1906 and the church had to close. St Peter's now stands in ruins whilst the nearby St Andrew's church remains in use.

'Burlingham. Gamekeepers House'

'South Burlingham Hall. Mr Read'
A stunning building that has not changed to this day. It is now called 'Old Hall Farm'.

Cantley

'Cantley Rectory. Rev William Gilbert & family'

Caister

'Roadside Inn Caister'
The Kings Arms Inn with a group of curious locals posing in the road.

'Caister House'
Croquet is being played on the lawn while the gardener waters the flowers, the maid serves tea and somebody looks on from the window. Everybody is perfectly posed to create a balanced composition.

'Caister Church from Yarmouth Road'.
What is now a very busy road junction was once an idyllic rural scene. The ghost of the dog beside the man's legs is as a result of a long exposure.

'Draining Mill. Caister Marshes 1860'.
This is an interesting record of early mill design, showing a post mill used to drain water from the dykes, at a sluice gate on the marshes.

Clippesby

'Clippesby Church Interior'
This is a rare interior shot taken by William Finch using beautiful natural light from the windows.

Filby

'Filby Wheelwrights Shop'

'Filby Fox & Hounds Public House'
With nine people, dressed in their Sunday best about to embark on a cart journey, comfort was not a high priority. The landlord of the 'Fox and Hounds' from 1869 to 1883 was Mr Charles Goodwin with his wife Matilda. The photographer's barrow can be seen in the background behind the horse.

Fishley

'Fishley New Rectory, Finch'
Fishley New Rectory was built between 1871 and 1881 by Miss Sophia Edwards of Hardingham who was the owner of Fishley Manor at this time. When this photograph was taken it was home to the Barry family. This huge, majestic house, with its many out buildings, is now 'The Amber Lodge', a restaurant and hotel standing just outside Acle.

Fleggburgh

'Burgh Flegg road side from'
The 'Kings Head' in Fleggburgh. This building was demolished around the turn of 20th century and was replaced by the current building. However the flint building in the corner can still are seen.

'Burgh Church and distant view of Rectory'
A beautifully composed shot with trees framing the distant cottages. Two curious women are looking on from the cottage door.

Freethorpe

'Freethorpe Walpoles New Alms Houses'
These bungalows had been built in 1871 by the Walpole family for widows over the age of 60. Their family crest is visible on the front of the building. The almshouses are still in use as such today.

Halvergate

'Halvergate - distant view of Church from Mr Lacon's grounds'.
Mr and Mrs Lacon are pictured here in the foreground with an unknown companion. The Lacon's house is now known as 'The Rookery'

'Halvergate – Mr Gillet's old farm'
Arthur Finch can be seen striking his usual pose in the foreground.

'Halvergate – old Mr Gillet. Has not been out of his house for 21 years. 1870'
A beautiful naturally lit portrait of Mr Gillet clutching a book. The reasons for his reclusive life are unknown but he had been a well respected farmer and his family were village benefactors. In 2010 a small close was built and named after him.

Hemsby

'Hemsby Hall Door. Mr Copemans'
Note Arthur Finch hiding in the shadows, unaware that he is in the photograph.

Moulton

'Moulton Blacksmiths Shop'
In 1881 the master blacksmith in Moulton was one Robert Gilbert who we suspect is portrayed here with his family.

Ormesby

'Ormesby Manor House, Mr Nelson'

Panxworth

'Panxworth Red Lion'
The landlord of the Red Lion in 1871 and 1881 was William Wright. The building is still there but it is no longer a pub. The post mill in the background was a two storey roundhouse that was accessed by a ladder. It was occupied by James Chapman and his family. This mill was blown down during a storm on 18th January 1881.

Reedham

'Reedham'
A group of local characters standing in front of a dutch gabled pub, probably 'The Brickmakers Arms'. The malting can be seen in the background and in the foreground is a slip way going down to the River Yare.

'Reedham. The Ship Inn'
Finch has taken this photograph from the same spot as the last image, but turning towards the 'Ship Inn'. The landlord is Richard Charles Mutten. Logs are being transported by horse to the steam saw mill that stood near the pub in 1877.

'Reedham. Making barrels for herring'
Barrel making for the Great Yarmouth herring fleet was a big local industry at this time.

'*Reedham Brickfields'*.
This was another local industry that was captured by Finch. The horse in the background would be turning the clay to make the bricks. The young man in the centre is black, which would be quite unusual in such a rural village at this time.

'Reedham. Birds eye view of Hall. Mrs Rose'.
An unusual view of the Old Hall taken from the church tower. It must have been quite a climb for Finch, carrying his camera equipment and glass plates to the top of the tower.

'Reedham Station. The Plate Layers'.
The railway arrived in Reedham in 1844. This is yet another beautiful group portrait showing Finch's artistic eye for balanced composition. The plate layers can be seen in the foreground and the full uniformed staff are in the background between their shoulders.

'Reedham Railway Station. Arrival of excursion train from Yarmouth'.
This is again wrongly captioned as it is in fact a goods train coming into the station, probably from the Norwich direction. The gentleman in the top hat may be Mr William Jackson who was the Station Master from 1861 to 1885.

'Reedham. Swing Bridge on Railway'.
Finch photographed the swing bridge in both its open and closed positions to the river traffic. In this image, a wherry can be seen to the left of the bridge and the vast expanse of marshland can be seen in the background. The young lad sitting by the railway line could once again be William's son Arthur.

Repps

'Repps – Mill'
Arthur Finch posing in front of the post mill. Repps post mill was built in 1805. At the time this photograph was taken the miller was John Addy. He continued at the mill until it blew down during a gale in 1895.

Rollesby

'Rollesby. Dr Waller'
A beautiful portrait of John Turpin Waller (1816-1894). Born in Cambridge, Doctor Waller married a local Stokesby woman, Mary Campbell who had sadly died by the time this photograph was taken.

'*Rollesby Blacksmiths Shop*'

There is definitely a theme within Finch's portfolio of works. He has photographed the blacksmith's shop in nearly every village. The Rollesby blacksmith and wheelwright was Richard S. Annison who was also the Parish Clerk. Note William Finch's thumb print on the left hand side.

'*Rollesby. Ensors (?) Farm after the fire*'.

Finch often photographed local events including devastating fires, as seen here. The letters C P E that are visible on the roof of the barn probably belonged to Charles Peploe Ensor. He died in 1897, being of Rollesby Hall and leaving the not insubstantial sum of £15,971 1s/ 1d.

'*Rollesby. Rev Tacon*'

Runham

'Runham Village'
Locals on the village green in front of the pond. The character in the foreground may be the village blacksmith.
The village pond no longer exists.

South Walsham

'South Walsham. New Iron Works'
Arthur Finch can once again be seen outside the new iron works. The building, that still stands today, was erected by Thomas Smithdale who supplied J. J. Colman with the machinery for mustard making in the mid 19th century. The Smithdales went on to make a few bad business decisions, firstly deciding to make their own mustard which, not surprisingly, lost them the machinery contract for Colman's. They also built their ironworks near South Walsham, predicting that the railway line would come this way. Instead it went via Acle where the family eventually moved in 1892.

'South Walsham'

Children playing street games outside the 'Ship Inn' which stands on the right of the road. The two church towers can be seen in the background. Apparently, two powerful and rivalling 11th century landlords, both built churches on the high ground of the village. It was not until 1971 that the tower of St Lawrence fell down.

'South Walsham Old Hall'

This photograph is actually of Manor Farm, a stunning and imposing newly thatched building.

Stokesby

'Stokesby Burnt Houses'.

'Stokesby Village'
This view is looking towards the green from outside the 'Ferry Inn'. The tower mill, built in 1827, is in the background.

'Stokesby School'
The new Stokesby school house that was built in 1876. The school house, now the 'Stokesby Community Centre', has changed little to this day.

'Stokesby – Birds eye view of Rectory'.
This is another aerial view taken from the Stokesby church tower. We can see the well tended vegetable gardens of the Rectory, built in 1840.

Strumpshaw

'Strumpshaw. House opposite pond. Mr Piles'.
A view looking across the pond towards a posed family group. Note the woman sitting side saddle on the pony.

Thrigby

'Thrigby Rectory'
A whiskered elderly gent stands outside the rectory which is now part of Thrigby Hall Wildlife Gardens. The Rectory, once the seat of Thomas William Daniel esq. J.P. was rebuilt in 1876 on the site of an ancient manse.

Thurne

'Thurne Hall'
Finch took great care in composing his subjects so that they could all be clearly seen. The lady of the house is in full riding dress on a horse. A servant is feeding the ducks and the groom is standing in the background. There is no distinction between the family and staff. The movement of the ducks shows a long exposure time.

Tunstall

'Tunstall Village Hay Makers'
The hay makers, all bearing rakes and scythes, toasting each other with a mug of ale. A group of onlookers can be seen in the background.

'*Tunstall. Stracey Arms, Yarmouth New Road*'
The Stracey Arms was a stopping point half way along the seven mile Acle New Road, known locally as the Acle Straight. The direct road between Acle and Great Yarmouth was built in 1831. At the time this photograph was taken, the landlord of the Stracey Arms was Scurrell Youngs. This building was demolished in the 1960s and was replaced with a modern building that still stands at this junction. Note Finch's cart against the pub wall.

'*Tunstall Church, interior of ruins*'
Arthur Finch is posing within the church ruins, part of which is still in use as a church today.

Upton

'Upton. Mr Parkin's (sic) House'
Two farm horses are pulling a seed drill through the village. Note the children's faces that can be seen behind the horse. This house is presently called the Hollies and looks little changed from this time.

Winterton

'Winterton – Church in the distance'

'Winterton. Three Mariners Inn'
This is probably a school party standing outside the local inn as the girls are all wearing their pinafore uniforms. Finch's photographic cart can be seen standing in the background against the wall. The walk to Winterton from Acle would have been at least 8 miles and must have been quite a journey.

Index of Photographs

Back cover
Mr Finch (Sig Henri Ægena) 1879
'Thetford Butchers Shop Darbyshire'